LOVINGLY GIVEN TO A FI
WITH DEEP AND LASTI

FROM:- YOUR (ANGLICAN) FRIEND.

†

POPE JOHN PAUL II

pilgrim of faith

WORDS
OF
INSPIRATION

◆

THE C. R. GIBSON COMPANY
Norwalk, Connecticut 06856

Copyright © 1987, 1984 by the K. S. GINIGER COMPANY, Inc.
Published by the C. R. GIBSON COMPANY
Norwalk, Connecticut 06856
All rights reserved
Printed in the United States of America
ISBN 0-8378-1829-X

"With firm faith,

renewed hope,

and ever deeper love."

POPE JOHN PAUL II

FOREWORD

"Nothing can give us a profound sense of the meaning of our earthly life... as can an inner attitude of seeing ourselves as pilgrims," writes Pope John Paul II in words quoted later in this book. And this remarkable man certainly sees himself as a pilgrim, not only figuratively but literally. His travels since his election to the Roman Catholic Church's highest office in 1978 have made him the most widely-traveled pontiff in the history of the Church. Pope John Paul II has carried his message to Catholics and non-Catholics, to Christians and non-Christians, on every continent. In the course of these voyages, he has made pilgrimages to many religious shrines. Some of the passages in this volume are taken from words spoken by him in the course of these journeys. The Vatican's annual directory lists John Paul II, of Cracow, Poland, as "universal pastor of the Church." His writings and speeches demonstrate that this is a role he has filled with great devotion and energy.

Karol Wojtyla was born in Wadowice, Poland, in 1920, was ordained a priest in 1946, taught moral theology and ethics at Polish universities until he was named Archbishop of Cracow in 1963, and was created a cardinal by Pope Paul VI in 1967. Poet and playwright as well as priest, he has some fifteen published works to his credit. He has always been interested in sports, especially skiing and rowing, but finds little time for them in his present busy schedule.

This selection of words taken from the Pope's writings, sermons, homilies and addresses is based on a more extensive selection made in the Vatican by Bishop Peter Canisius Johannes van Lierde, O. S. A., Vicar General of his Holiness for Vatican City, and translated from the original languages by the late Firmin O'Sullivan, published in English as *Prayers and Devotions from Pope John Paul II* in 1984.

That daily devotional quotes the Pope, on the occasion of his first pastoral visit to the Americas, as saying to the people of the United States:

"It is a great joy for me... to greet all the American people of every race, color and creed. From so many quarters—Catholics, Protestants and Jews—America has opened her heart to me. And, on my part, I come to you, America, with sentiments of friendship, reverence and esteem. I come as one who already knows you and loves you, as one who wishes to fulfill completely your noble destiny of service to the world... I feel close to all of you, and you are all in my prayers."

His messages of faith, hope and love, found in the pages that follow, offer the reader a share in those prayers.

Kenneth Seeman Giniger
Editor

MESSAGES OF FAITH

◆

We Are All Pilgrims

Nothing can give us a profound sense of
the meaning of our earthly life and stimu-
late us to live it as a brief experimental
stage—as can an inner *attitude of seeing ourselves as pilgrims.*

◇

It is not enough to accept passively those
riches of the faith which are handed
down in your tradition and by your
culture. A treasure is entrusted, talents
are offered, which ought to be accepted
with responsibility, so that they may bear
fruit in abundance.

Mary said: "I am the servant of the Lord. Let it be done to me as you say" (*Lk* 1: 38). And, with these words, she expressed what was *the fundamental attitude of her life: her faith!* Mary believed! She trusted in God's promises and was faithful to His will. All her earthly life was a "pilgrimage of faith." For, like us, she walked in shadows and hoped for things unseen... This woman of faith, Mary of Nazareth, the mother of God, has been given to us as *a model in our pilgrimage of faith.* From Mary, we learn to surrender to God's will in all things.

◇

You receive the gift of the Holy Spirit so that you may work with deep faith and with abiding charity, so that you may help to bring to the world the fruits of reconciliation and peace.

We live our faith when we are open to
God's coming, when we persevere in His
advent.

◇

The attitude of spirit befitting the be-
liever is an attitude of vigilance, the ex-
pression of spiritual aspiration to God
through faith.

◇

Always have the courage and pride of your faith.
Deepen it. *Get close to Christ, ceaselessly,* as
living stones in the cornerstone, sure of
reaching the goal of your faith, the salvation of your souls.

Faith In A Difficult Age

We have so much need of faith! Great faith is so necessary to men of our time, the difficult modern age. Great faith is necessary today to individual families, communities, the Church.

◇

This epoch of ours requires from us Christians: "Faith plain to see and courageous, faith full of hope, faith living through love."

◇

A faith which is translated into lifestyle according to the Gospel, that is to say, a way of living which reflects the Beatitudes, shows itself in love, as the key to human existence, and adds power to the values of the person, to commit the person to solving the human problems of our time.

Our daily lives are in danger of experiencing—actually do experience—cases of inner pollution. But contact in faith with the word of the Lord purifies us, elevates us and gives us back energy.

◇

Only he who accepts his intellectual and moral *limits* and recognizes that he *needs* salvation can attain to faith and in faith meet, in Christ, his Redeemer.

◇

Faith... in its relation with culture, presents itself as a clarification of God's project, as an aid and complement to rationality. But rationality is not impoverished by having recourse to the Faith.

To Those Who Struggle:

Christian expectation: Perseverance in faith and in struggle.

◇

Truth, like Jesus Christ, may always be denied, persecuted, embattled, wounded, martyred, crucified; but it always lives again and rises again and cannot be wrenched out of the human heart.

◇

The reality of faith, of hope and of charity, the reality of suffering sanctified and sanctifying, the reality of the presence of the mother of God in the mystery of Christ and His Church on earth are a presence which is particularly alive in... the sick and the suffering.

◇

I thank God for the lives of all those who, wherever they be, suffer for their faith in God.

Look With The Eyes Of Faith

Let us look now with "the eyes of faith" to Christ's kingdom, and repeat, "May Your reign come."

◇

The more man lets himself be carried away by the eloquence of creatures, their richness and beauty, the more need to adore the Creator grows in him.

◇

Genuine faith: It is absolute dedication to things which are not seen, but which are capable of filling and ennobling a whole life.

◇

The ways of knowledge [are] through faith, for only such knowledge of the faith disposes the understanding to *union with the living God*.

God the Father's plan of salvation em-
braces all mankind; His one same Holy
Spirit is sent as a gift to all who are open
to receive Him in faith.

◇

Let us persevere in asking the Holy Spirit
to remove all divisions from our faith, to
give us the perfect unity in truth and love
for which Christ prayed; for which Christ
died.

◇

The soul—the more it will have faith, so
much the more will it be united to God.

I exhort you to be courageous now and always, without becoming bewildered by difficulties, and always trusting in Him who is your Friend and your Redeemer, and watching and praying to keep your faith sound and your grace lively.

◇

Pause and give thanks to God for the unique culture and rich human tradition which you have inherited and for the greatest gift anyone can receive, the gift of faith.

◇

Prayer

We ask Almighty God to renew the face of the earth through the life-giving power of the Spirit. Send forth Your Spirit, O Lord, renew our hearts and minds with the gifts of light and truth. Renew Your Church on earth with the gifts of penance and reconciliation, with unity in faith and love.

MESSAGES OF HOPE

◆

Everything Is New!

When you meet Christ in prayer, when you get to know His Gospel and reflect on it in relation to your hopes and your plan for the future, then everything is new.

◇

In the cross lies hope of a Christian renewal..., but only if Christians themselves take the message of the cross seriously.

◇

The Lord is always with you... to give all the regenerative power of His Gospel, of His grace and of His love. Never ignore Him! Never put Him aside!

Christ rose again so that man may retrieve the authentic meaning of existence, *so that man may live his life fully*, that man, who comes *from God*, may live *in God*.

◇

What is the truth which penetrates and enlivens us today? What message does the Church, our Mother, announce? The message of hope.

◇

Behold the day of universal hope, the day on which all human sufferings, disappointments, humiliations, crosses, violated human dignity, disrespected human life, all are gathered up and associated with the Risen One.

Be Heralds Of Hope!

Men and women of deep and abiding faith: Be heralds of hope. Be messengers of joy. Be true workers for justice.

This is the certainty of which the world had need, the world in which the apostles preached the Gospel of Christ; this is the hope of Him of whom humanity in our time has need, those to whom we would communicate the message: Christ is risen and by rising again He has broken what seemed and still seems to many an implacable vortex of decadence, degradation and corruption in history.

They live without true joy because they live without hope.

◊

They live without hope because they have never heard, really heard, the Good News of Jesus Christ, because they have never met a brother or a sister who touched their lives with the love of Jesus and lifted them up from their misery.

◊

Prayer becomes a need of the soul: "In prayer the heart alters and in this conversion the inner eye becomes pure." Pray in hope, pray with faith and love. Prayer is as necessary as the grace it obtains for us.

◊

We must... become more and more united with Christ, therefore more united among ourselves in Christ. He alone... can bring our hopes to fulfillment.

Deep truth, truth which converts, re-
stores hope, puts everything in its place,
reconciles and lets optimism arise.

◇

Indispensable to today's diplomacy is to
justify the hopes that are placed in it: the
ever deeper insertion of the supreme values of the moral and spiritual order into
the aims of peoples and into the methods
used in pursuit of these aims.

◇

Only through acceptance of the Gospel
can every hope. . . find full realization.

◇

Death has its limits. Christ has opened up
a great hope: the hope of life beyond the
sphere of death.

Our Light Of Hope

Have humble and courageous awareness of what the Father has given you. Let this awareness be your strength, your light, your hope.

◇

The divine wisdom is that *sublime science* which preserves the savor of salt, so that it will not become tasteless: which feeds the light of the lamp, so that it may light up the depths of the human heart, guide its secret yearnings, its seeking and its hopes.

◇

Faith, based on the Gospel story, tells us that God became man. That is, He entered into human history, not so much to challenge it as to *enlighten* it, to *orient* it, to *save* it, by redeeming every single soul. This is the meaning of the Incarnation of the Word; this is the authentic meaning of Christmas, the feast of true joy and true hope.

May the light of hope reveal itself to all.

◇

In spite of all, there is hope and joy, because God became man, because Christ was really incarnated for us, the Savior announced by the prophets came, and has remained with us!

◇

With the Church's liturgy, we may greet the cross as "the only hope" and source of grace and pardon.

◇

Prayer

Lord, may Your grace be upon us, because we hope in You.

MESSAGES OF LOVE

◆

God's Constant Love

What really matters in life is that we are loved by Christ and that we love Him in return. In comparison with the love of Jesus, everything else is secondary. And, without the love of Jesus, everything else is useless.

◇

It is exactly this God of our Advent: the Creator and Redeemer, who makes the profession of such love for man, for man the sinner: "Though the mountains leave their place, and the hills be shaken, my love will never leave you" (*Is* 54: 10).

◇

The more we purify our souls, the more shall we make room for God's love in our hearts, the more Christ will be able to come and be born in us!

Jesus Christ is a "king who loves." Because He loved us humans to the shedding of His blood. Because He loves, He has liberated us from sin, because only love is capable of freeing us from sin.

◇

Only love creates good, and, in the last analysis, it alone can be perceived in all dimensions and profiles in created things and in man above all.

◇

We must measure man according to the gauge of the conscience, with the measure of the spirit open to God. Only the Holy Spirit can fill up this heart, that is, lead it to self-realization through love and wisdom.

◇

Blessed be God, rich in mercy, for the great love with which He has loved us!

We Are Called To Love

God created man in His image and like-
ness by calling him into existence *for love's
sake*; at the same time He called him *to love*.
God is love and lives a mystery of personal communion of love in Himself....
Love is the fundamental and native voca-
tion of every human being.

◇

There are always souls to enlighten, sin-
ners to pardon, tears to dry, disappointments to console, sick to encourage,
children and youngsters to guide. There
is, there ever shall be, man to love and
save, in Christ's name!

Man lives in the full dimension of his humanity only when he is capable of *surpassing himself with the power of truth and love.*

◇

We receive the Holy Spirit, that the power of truth and love may form our interior life and make it radiate outwardly as well.

◇

A Christian who has not learned to see and love Christ in his neighbor is not fully Christian. We are our brothers' keepers; we are bound to each other by the bond of love.

We must love others with the same love which God pours into our hearts and with which He Himself loves us.

◇

Love which is directed to man actually always finds its ultimate source in God, who is love.

◇

Mother of beautiful love, pray for us! Teach us to love God and our brethren, as you have loved them. Cause our love for others to be ever patient, benign, respectful.

Love Can Change The World

Believing in the crucified Son means "seeing the Father," means believing that love is present in the world and that this love is more powerful than any kind of evil in which individuals, humanity, or the world is involved.... Mercy is an indispensable dimension of love; it is, as it were, love's second name and, at the same time, the specific manner in which love is revealed and effected vis-a-vis the reality of the evil that is in the world.

◊

The message of the Beatitudes [is] the message of love for God and one's neighbor, the message of moral commitment to the authentic transformation of society.

The experience of the past and of our own time shows that justice alone is not enough; indeed, it can lead to negation and annihilation of itself, unless *that deeper force which is love* is allowed to shape human living in its various dimensions.

◇

Say "No" to death, to hatred, to violence, to terror, to error, to evil, to degradation. Say "Yes" to the good, to the beautiful, to truth, to justice, to responsibility, to life, to peace, to love.

◇

The Gospel... urges us *to share every one of man's situations and conditions,* with a passionate love for everything to do with his condition of being a creature of God's.

Love for mankind, for all mankind, without any exception or division at all: without difference of race, of culture, of language, of concept of the world, without distinction between friends and enemies. This is love for mankind and it desires every true good for each member of mankind.

◇

The deepest spring of man's spiritual development is found in the evangelical commandment of love.

◇

Let us persevere in asking the Holy Spirit to remove all divisions from our faith, to give us the perfect unity in truth and love for which Christ prayed, for which Christ died.

A Touch Of Eternal Love

The cross is like a touch of eternal love upon the most painful wounds of man's earthly existence.

◇

Our reconciliation with God, the return to the Father's house, is accomplished through Christ. His suffering and death on the cross stand between every human conscience, every human sin, and the Father's boundless love. Such love is prompt to rise up and pardon; it is nothing else than mercy.

◇

God's salvation is the work of a love greater than man's sin. Love alone can wipe out sin and liberate from sin. Love alone can consolidate man in the good, in the unalterable and eternal good.

The world and man *were consecrated through the power of the redemption.* They were consecrated to Him who is infinitely holy. They were offered and confided to Love Himself, to the merciful Love.

◇

Every epoch—past, present, and to come—produces shining examples of the power which is in Jesus Christ for the edification of all... to give testimony of the primacy of love in the world.

◇

There is a pledge of satisfaction for that burning thirst for happiness and love which everyone bears in himself and herself, in the secret of the heart.

The Blessings Of Married Love

Love that is not a passing emotion—temporary infatuation—but a responsible and free decision to bind oneself completely, "in good times and in bad," to one's partner… is the gift of oneself to the other.

◇

Conjugal love entails a totality where all components of the person, the claims of the body and of the instincts, the power of feeling and affection, the aspirations of the spirit and of the will, all enter in. It aims at a profoundly personal unity, that which goes beyond union in one flesh and leads to making but one heart and one soul.

◇

Sexuality is realized in a truly human way only if it is an integral part of the love with which the man and the woman commit themselves to each other until death.

Love, reinforced by the grace of the sacrament of matrimony, shall show itself to be stronger than any weakness and every crisis through which our families pass at times.

◇

In its deepest reality, love is essentially giving and, while conjugal love leads the spouses to reciprocal "knowledge" which makes them "one flesh," it does not end within the couple; it makes them capable of the greatest possible giving whereby they become cooperators with God for the gift of life and a new human person. So, while the spouses give to each other, they give the reality of the child out beyond themselves, as a living reflection of their love, a permanent sign of married unity and a living and inseparable synthesis of their being father and mother.

To Families

The parents' love turns from being *source* to *soul*, then into *norm*, inspiring and guiding the whole of the concrete work of education, and enriching it with those values of gentleness, constancy, goodness, service, and spirit of sacrifice, which are the most precious fruit of love.

◇

Parental love is called to become the visible sign to the children of God's own love, that of Him "from whom all fatherhood in heaven and on earth is named."

◇

We must reach out with love—the love of Christ—to those who know the pain of failure in marriage; to those who know the loneliness of bringing up a family on their own.

The church sees in the face of women the reflection of a beauty which mirrors the loftiest sentiments of which the human heart is capable: the self-offering totality of love; the strength that is capable of bearing the greatest sorrows; the limitless fidelity and tireless devotion to work; the ability to combine penetrating intuition with words of support and encouragement.

◇

The family is the community of love and life. So the mystery of human life was entrusted to it by the Creator. Matrimony is the beginning of the new community of love and life upon which man's future on earth depends.

It is in *conjugal and family love* that the Christian family's participation in the prophetical, priestly and kingly mission of Jesus Christ and His Church is realized.

◇

The family has the mission of becoming ever more what it is, that is, a community of life and love.

◇

Prayer

Jesus Christ, Son of the Living God, grant that... all of us may love You more, as in ourselves we live the mysteries of Your life again, from the conception and birth up to the cross and the resurrection.

Edited by Kenneth S. Giniger
Book design by John DiLorenzo
Type set in Weiss and Weiss Italic
Cover design by Ralph DiMarco